Engaging and Challenging Curriculum: Supporting Advanced and Gifted Learners

Jennifer G. Beasley, Christine Briggs,
Leighann Pennington, and Marcia B. Imbeau

Cheryll M. Adams, Series Editor

National Association for Gifted Children
1331 H Street, NW, Suite 1001
Washington, DC 20005
202-785-4268
http://www.nagc.org

TABLE OF CONTENTS

INTRODUCTION

The need for clarity concerning exemplary curricula for advanced learners continues to be a priority for education. With the adoption of the Common Core State Standards (CCSS) in many states, a new conversation has evolved around meeting the needs of students for whom the "standard" curriculum may not be a good fit. But no conversation about high quality curriculum for gifted learners can take place without consideration of quality curriculum in general. Hence, one purpose of this book is to highlight criteria for high quality curriculum. Then we will define the key features of curriculum for gifted and talented students in light of those criteria and the current knowledge about curriculum for gifted students. Finally, this book will provide exemplars in curriculum from the field of gifted and talented that can serve as a guide for curriculum selection.

Student achievement and teacher accountability underlie the quest to prepare K-12 students for college, careers, and competition in the global market. To respond to these goals, developers of CCSS and the accompanying assessments created benchmarks of students' success in meaningfully grappling with rigor, relevance, and relationships within and across content disciplines. The transition process from individual state standards to the Common Core acknowledges the excellent foundation states have laid, and proponents of the CCSS view them as a next step in providing all students with a high quality education. The goal of the standards is to be clear about the benchmarks for success that define college and career readiness so that those benchmarks can be understood by

every student, parent, and teacher
(http://www.corestandards.org/the-standards).

However, the CCSS, like any set of state standards, are not a curriculum. They are a set of shared goals and expectations for student outcomes. The National Governors Association and the Council of Chief State School Officers[1] stated in their Myths v. Facts About the Common Core Standards, "teachers will need to continue to devise lesson plans and tailor instruction to the individual needs of the students in their classrooms" (p.4).

Curriculum, in contrast to standards, has many components and can be regarded in many different ways. For some educators, it refers to the overall content of what is to be taught. For others, curriculum describes the underlying principles of the teaching and learning approach. And for still others it refers to both content and instructional principles by defining the overall "what," "how," and "why" of teaching. It is that final definition of curriculum that we will expand on here as we identify the key elements of curriculum for gifted and talented learners.

BEST PRACTICES DEFINED

What does it mean to create curriculum in response to learner traits? What is "good" curriculum? In a meta-analysis of research, John Hattie[2] noted that the content of curricula was less important to student success than the strategies teachers use to implement the curriculum. Best practices that stand out as critical to student achievement tend to center around:

- selection of learning strategies that enable students to construct meaning,
- implementation of practices that are planned, deliberate, and explicit,
- balancing surface knowledge and deep understanding, and
- using ongoing assessment to identify and eliminate misconceptions.

In order for practices to be transformational to student understanding, they must be implemented in a community that is student-centered. The National Research Council[3] found common themes in transformational learning environments, including that they are learner-centered, knowledge-centered, assessment-centered, and community-centered. For all learners, having a nurturing, safe environment in which to learn and grow is key to achievement. As the key features of challenging curriculum are defined, educators must keep in mind that what students learn is situated in a community. Relationships cannot be sacrificed for content; community is foundational.

Challenging curriculum must build upon best practices for teaching and learning when serving the needs of advanced students. In the field of gifted education, curriculum has been a foundational element that has been expanded, explored, and researched. In the next section, the key features found in challenging curriculum are defined in the context of gifted education.

KEY FEATURES OF CHALLENGING CURRICULUM

Building upon best practices and defining challenging curriculum requires differentiating curriculum to meet the needs of advanced learners. Key features in challenging curriculum should be evident in all curricula; that is, all students should be appropriately challenged. Curriculum for the general population of students may need to be adjusted to respond to gifted learners. The features noted in this publication are rooted in curriculum models from the field of gifted education. For example, Sandra Kaplan's[4] work is evident throughout. For more information on exemplary models in gifted education, look to the key resources section at the end of the publication. Each key feature for challenging curriculum is briefly discussed and illustrated.

Differentiation

Sandra Kaplan[5] states that in order to meet the characteristics/needs of gifted students, differentiated learning experiences should incorporate greater depth and complexity into the core curriculum. Depth is defined in her work as the process of focusing on more difficult, divergent, abstract qualities of knowing a discipline or content area. Complexity is defined as knowledge being extended so students identify associations, connections, relationships, and links within and across disciplines.

One way to gain greater levels of depth and complexity within a content area is for students to have learning experiences that require them to explore key ideas (core content) using appropriately advanced critical/creative thinking skills. When students also routinely use the skills of professionals in the field of study to ultimately develop a product or performance to demonstrate learning, they are likely attaining greater depth of knowledge and complexity of understanding. When students are engaged in abstract thinking, asked to consider many possibilities, and must defend their decisions, high-level learning is in place.

Carol Tomlinson[6] asserts that diverse learners, including those who are most advanced, should encounter learning experiences designed to address their varying readiness, interests, and learner profile needs. Effective teachers design instruction aimed at a student's zone of proximal development (ZPD as defined by Vygotsky). Instruction in a student's ZPD occurs when tasks offered to particular learners are not too hard, not too easy but just difficult enough that the student must exert cognitive energy to successful master the outcome. When teachers ensure that all students are challenged, the most advanced learners are pushed so that new learning takes place and growth occurs. Further, instruction tied to students' interests can be particularly motivating for learners where persistence in studying a topic in-depth is promoted. Lastly, when teachers allow students to work in ways that are most comfortable for them, teachers may find that students' enjoyment in learning increases and new talents may be revealed. These approaches are most successful when:

- a supportive learning environment is present,
- clear learning goals focusing on student engagement and understanding are selected,
- continual assessment of students' proximity to the learning goals is routine,
- instruction is consistently adjusted based on assessment data, and

- flexibility is common when managing the classroom.

When making curricular decisions, the current learning status and speed at which a gifted student is progressing may suggest that acceleration and enrichment opportunities are a good fit for particular learners. Acceleration could mean moving faster through content or skill acquisition. It could also mean subject acceleration, grade skipping, or early admission to college. Enrichment allows students to explore topics of interest, make connections to units of study, or design projects that provide a service to a real-world audience.

A strategy recommended by Renzulli and Reis[7] that incorporates both enrichment and acceleration is curriculum compacting. Teachers who use this strategy identify the knowledge and skills already mastered by a student and replace planned knowledge and skill instruction with alternate tasks including enrichment opportunities that provide activities requiring deeper inquiry into a topic, or acceleration to move to more complex elements of a task to promote continued learning. Curriculum for the gifted should have embedded alternatives to meet the enrichment and acceleration needs gifted students may require.

In Practice
An example of curriculum compacting in the classroom could be as simple as providing all students in a math class with the opportunity to do the "5 hardest first." The math teacher would select five problems that really provide evidence that the student understood the skills or concepts in the lesson. If students were willing and able to do those five problems correctly, they would not have to do the rest of the assignment. Students who finished early could pursue

an engaging independent project or task that would extend or enhance what was being learned in the classroom.

Opportunities for Talent Development

Curriculum for the gifted should provide opportunities for talent development. Exposing students to new ideas, asking questions to identify areas of interest, and providing venues for student-designed products provides a rich context to watch students and see how they rise to the challenge. Renzulli[8] talks about developing talent and notes gifted behavior can appear in certain people, at certain times, under certain conditions. As teachers we want to find curriculum that provides a variety of student-centered learning experiences and supports the development of student talent.

In curriculum, talent development might appear as an opportunity for a student to engage in an activity that is aligned with his or her strengths, learning preferences, or interests. A lesson might provide a student a chance to explore advanced content or acquire skills, methodologies, and dispositions of the practicing professional. These opportunities not only challenge learners, but are a way for educators to learn more about students' strengths and how to better meet their needs.

In Practice

In one Science, Technology, Engineering, and Math (STEM) magnet school, teachers in the primary grades designed one of their first units to give students opportunities for talent development, but also to identify students with strengths in those fields. For this unit, it was important that the students understand that:

- We interact and improve the world around us through inquiry and problem solving.
- There are particular skills, knowledge, and tools that are associated with STEM.
- STEM prepares us for the 21st century and enables us to be lifelong learners.
- STEM provides a framework for solving everyday problems to improve the quality of life.

As a part of the unit, kindergarten and first-grade students could choose one way to communicate what they know about STEM and what it means to them. Students could choose from the following products: a song, a slideshow to be shown on the school's welcome screen, a welcome letter to new students, or an advertisement for the school. Each product was designed to be open-ended and also targeted toward the learning goals for the unit. An example of one of the choices follows:

Imagine our school had just started its first year as a STEM school. In honor of our new school, you have been asked to write a song that the school will sing in class as well as in school assemblies. You have been learning about how we interact and improve the world around us, that there are particular skills and knowledge that are associated with STEM, that STEM prepares us for lifelong learning and can help us solve everyday problems. Your task is to create a song that represents our school and what we do as we learn about STEM. Your song should have a tune and words that would be easy for us to sing in class. You might use a tune that is familiar to others (ex: Row, Row, Row Your Boat!), but your words (lyrics) need to help us understand what we have learned about our STEM school.

In all of the activities the teachers should take great care that the same content, skills, and understandings were reflected to ensure the learning goals were achieved.

Clarity and Nature of Goals

When creating curriculum, educators must make sure that they are aware of the destination. Standards are a starting point, but they do not help clarify for teachers and their students the "why" behind the lesson or unit. Inherent in the goals of a unit of study is purpose for learning. What students learn must be rigorous, but also relevant. In order to do this, the goals selected for units of study should be anchored around the big ideas of the discipline. Big ideas are really another way to describe what principles and concepts drive the discipline being taught in the classroom. For instance, some examples of big ideas in history might be:

- Competent historical research requires the location and interpretation of documentary evidence.
- A successful democracy depends on the participation of its citizens.
- People migrate in order to meet basic needs.

As the examples suggest, those ideas should be centered on specific principles and concepts that illuminate the discipline so that in-depth study is possible and the learning is long-lasting. Designing curriculum focused on the key concepts and principles requires teachers to study their discipline to determine which understandings (principles) are most salient for the topic under study and would push students to use key knowledge and skills in ways that allow students to grow in expertise. Curriculum developed in this manner also requires teachers to create assessments and learning opportunities that focus on understanding rather than on discrete skills that are unrelated to the important learning goals. Therefore the goals for a quality unit of study would include the most important knowledge, understanding, and skill that would allow students to have clarity about what they were learning and why it was important.

Being clear about curricular goals means that educators must be clear about the disciplines associated with the unit or lesson. Incorporating the concepts, principles, skills, methodologies, and dispositions into the learning may mean that teachers examine the content more closely.

In Practice

An example of applying the notion of big ideas might be transforming a typical unit about state history[9] into an exploration of how our study of state history reveals the identity of a particular place and people. Key goals for such a unit might be:

- Culture helps us to understand ourselves as both individuals and members of various groups.
- Our identity is shaped by the actions we take, the traits that help define who we are, and the choices that we make.
- The study of state history reveals the identity of a particular place and people.
- Humans seek to understand their historical roots and to locate themselves in time.
- Public historians use a set of tools and methods in their research to profile, chronicle, and communicate about the history of people.
- Public history is a way to transform the two-dimensional to three-dimensional.

11

- The study of history helps people see change over time.
- The perspective of the historian impacts the interpretation of history.

Instead of limiting the unit to just the facts about a state, the unit can be constructed so the students study the state through the perspective of public historians, who are experts in communicating the history of people. Clarity and nature of the objectives help teachers and students reach deeper into the disciplines being studied, which can result in a richer, more transformational learning experience.

Evaluation

Evaluating student progress must be strategically embedded in any quality curriculum. As Wiggins and McTighe[10] suggest, begin with the end in mind. In designing strategies for evaluating student growth, teachers start with identifying the outcome goals for learning at the same time as they design the assessments to measure the degree to which these goals are met. These two tools—goals and assessments—are essential in any curriculum used with students, particularly gifted students. In addition, assessment should be both formative and summative. Modification of instruction based on formative assessment reflects our understanding that some students may learn more quickly and some may struggle with a particular concept or skill—even if s/he is gifted. Types of assessments used in a unit could include product rubrics/checklists, observation tally sheets, student-teacher discussion and conversations, student self-reflections, and testing results. Any assessment used with a curriculum also should be a tool for the teacher to inform future planning. Group organization, task assignments, and small-group instruction should all be based on students' assessment data. If we start with where we want all learners to end up, as identified by standards, and measure progress through assessments, we are much more likely to create tasks and assessments that are aligned to our learning goals, which greatly benefit all students' learning.

Knowledge about all forms of assessment is essential for educators of students with gifts and talents. It is integral to identification, assessing each student's learning progress, and evaluation of programming. Educator understanding of non-biased, technically adequate, and equitable approaches enables them to identify students from diverse backgrounds. Gathering information from multiple types of assessments allows all students to demonstrate their strengths. Educators can also differentiate their curriculum and instruction based on traditional paper-and-pencil assessments, performance-based, product-based, and out-of-level assessments. As a result of each educator's use of ongoing assessments, students with gifts and talents demonstrate advanced and complex learning. Using these data, educators can then evaluate services and make adjustments to one or more of the school's programming components so that student performance is improved.

In Practice

At the onset of planning a unit, a teacher may want to think about some of the key assessments that he or she might embed in the unit of study. For example, a teacher getting ready to teach a unit on argumentative writing may want to pre-assess students to find out how his or her students organize their writing and whether they can use the structure of their writing to convey their opinion based upon evidence. During the pre-assessment, the teacher may ask the class to write on one side of the page and defend a particular perspective in the form of a paragraph and on the other side of the page identify topic ideas that interest them. Through the pre-assessment the teacher is not only gathering data on the students' writing skills, but also what interests them so that the teacher can choose assignments that attend to student readiness and interest.

Learning Activities

Learning experiences should be tailored to the learning needs of students. In order for students to grapple with the depth and complexity of ideas learning experiences must be:

- student centered,
- open-ended, problem-based with real-world applications,
- focused on developing higher level thinking skills, and
- engaging to students based on learning preferences and profiles.

Successful learning experiences are flexible so teachers can adjust tasks to fit the needs of their students. A variety of different, challenging, and interesting assignments should be offered to students incorporating options for real-world application or problem solving. Students should have the opportunity to develop creative and/or authentic products. When selecting learning activities for gifted and talented learners, following the *Could, Should, Would* principle[11] can be a guide for decision-making. *Could* all students participate in the learning activity? *Should* all students participate in the learning activity? *Would* all students participate in the learning activity? If the answer is "yes" to all three, then the activity is good for all students, not just for gifted learners.

In Practice

Performance tasks are one type of learning activity that can be a rich context for student exploration. An example from a fourth-grade unit on state history provided students with an opportunity to "Make History Public." The following is the example of the task:

Our state is getting ready to open a museum that will celebrate our state's history. For this project, you will take on the role of creating a museum exhibit that communicates to others the identity of our state. Each of you will have a chance to apply for a position at the museum: museum curator, public historian, exhibit designer, or museum docent. Together you will design one exhibit that you feel symbolizes our state identity.

Fourth-grade students rose to the challenge and interviewed for positions at the museum, each team created an exhibit based upon what they had been learning through the unit. The outcomes of this event were creative and gave the teacher many opportunities for identifying talent within her classroom.

Instructional Strategies

Experts in the field of gifted education suggest using a wide variety of instructional strategies to engage and challenge gifted students. The instructional strategies selected by the teacher should develop critical and creative thinking. The strategies chosen for gifted children should not just communicate content—they should lead students to understand and apply the concepts of a discipline and ask students to solve a problem authentic to the discipline. As you choose instructional strategies, keep in mind the characteristics of gifted students; often many gifted students thrive on making connections between ideas and dealing with abstraction. However, also remember to use differentiated instruction to tailor your teaching strategies to the individual learners in your classroom.

It is not necessarily about which instructional methods you choose, but rather how you use them. The instructional methods should be selected in the service of teaching students about the big-ideas, sophisticated concepts, and complex methodologies of the discipline and learning to think and work in expert-like ways. Some methods in particular, such as inductive reasoning, Socratic questioning, and perspective taking, can lead to rich and rigorous learning experiences for gifted students.

In Practice

Inductive reasoning requires students to be part of a constructive learning experience while arriving at big understandings or principles of the unit on their own, which can later be reinforced by the teacher. This instructional method might pair well with a lesson about bias and primary and secondary sources in history or an investigative unit in biology class.

Socratic questioning requires critical-thinking skills as students are asked to approach issues in an open-ended manner, to tolerate ambiguity, and remain open to posing questions instead of searching for one correct answer. Socratic seminars are often successful in the literature and history classrooms. To extend learning, some gifted students can be trained by the teacher to lead their own Socratic seminars, which develops leadership skills and intrapersonal intelligence.

Perspective taking is another instructional strategy that challenges gifted students and exhibits the criteria of critical and creative thinking that you should consider when selecting instructional methods for gifted learners. Abstract thinking, dealing with multiple perspectives, crafting an argument, critical and creative thinking, and employing methods of persuasion are required when students engage with this method of instruction. For example, in a science class, half of the students might be asked to take a pro-stem cell research stance, while the other half would take the opposite stance. They would conduct research, evaluate available data, and formulate and deliver convincing arguments; then students would be asked to switch sides and take the opposite perspective, researching, evaluating, and crafting arguments. This is a significantly more challenging than tackling only one side of an issue, and would be authentic to the experience of a research biologist who is asked to write an article or speak in a debate about a controversial issue; he or she needs to understand both sides of the issue to effectively construct an argument and refute the opposing argument. In this way, the instructional method chosen is authentic to the discipline and prepares students to lead to an authentic product or performance.

These are only a few examples; in a well-planned unit, a variety of instructional strategies will work in concert with the content to lead to authentic products.

Products

Products for gifted students should be as authentic to the discipline as possible; they also should be aligned to the standards, concepts, and principles that form the foundation of the unit in which they are embedded. Products are defined as "...performances or work samples created by students that provide evidence of student learning"[12]. Products can act as forms of ongoing assessment that showcase short-term or daily learning or serve as culminating evidence for what students know, understand, and can do as a result of participating in a unit. When planning a unit, consider using backwards design: design the final product before starting the unit and create lessons and experiences that scaffold and support students so they will be prepared to create the final product with high levels of expertise.

With preparation during the unit and teacher support, students will be able to create authentic products that require them to think and work in expert-like ways in order to create the product. The teacher should also invite experts in a field or mentors to assist in creating or assessing the final products.

If possible, students should be given some choice in how they complete the final product, which will spark interest and investment. Once again ensure the product choice includes attention to the learning outcomes and that the skills needed for high quality product production are included as learning objectives as well as learning activities. Keep in mind that PowerPoint and related products are very limited as real-life products. Products should be equitable and respectful of the work students have invested so far in the unit and the prior knowledge they possess. Among the range of choices, the products should be equally interesting and appealing to students while working toward the concepts, principles, and skills of the unit as a whole. In creating product tasks it is critical to consider the criteria on which the product will be assessed.

In Practice
One meaningful product assignment, portfolios for art and writing courses, often show evidence of student growth over time and also can include a valuable component that

asks students to reflect and self-evaluate. Self-assessment is an important component of a high quality product for gifted students.

Involving an audience of experts can make product assignments more meaningful. In writing class, this might mean creating a newspaper or submitting student writing to a literary magazine or local newspaper. In a physical science class, students could take part in a problem-based unit and conduct a town hall meeting about an important issue like drought, with students acting in the roles of hydrologists, public water officials, and community members; concerned citizens, science experts, and local public officials could be invited to take part in the meeting. In history class, students working on an oral history unit could create a website modeled after an exemplary website curated by an actual historian, using photos and audio files and other curated content from interviews with real people; then ask a historian to review the website. All of these product assignments could be authentic, meaningful, and motivating for gifted students; when embedded in a unit with strong concepts and principles, and allow students to engage deeply with the content and concepts of the unit as well as with the methodologies of a discipline.

Resources and Student Engagement

High quality units for gifted students should include a diverse and engaging assortment of resources. Resources should be made available that require students to interact at varying levels of challenge, so that students can extend their knowledge. Resources can be selected based on student interest, readiness level, and learning profile. Multi-faceted, multimedia resources should appeal to students and their various preferred mode of acquiring information and can lead to interactive experiences for individual students or groups of learners. While textbooks and other print materials are readily available, teachers of gifted students should take the next step to truly engage students with more varied resources. When encouraging gifted learners to think like a professional in a discipline, primary sources are particularly important; analyzing primary sources often requires students to use higher level, abstract-thinking skills.

In Practice

An example of accessing resources is found in a Parallel Curriculum Model unit[13] called "Experience Poetry." The unit includes interviews with poets about the writing process and requires students to analyze them as primary sources so that students can understand what inspires poets. Varied resources were used, including audio files/readings of poems, poetry texts at several levels of challenge, film clips, musical selections, and photos. These resources were strategically employed to reinforce the concepts, principles, and skills the unit was designed to address.

Resources should be thoughtfully integrated into the unit as a whole and used as part of extension activities for learners to move deeper into the principles and concepts of the unit. Overall, resources should be used in an authentic manner as tools to solve problems and answer questions relevant to the discipline

Curricular Alignment

Joyce VanTassel-Baska[14] emphasizes a need for curriculum balance calling for organized alignment across teachers within a district. The balance process requires a vertical teaming effort from elementary through secondary programs. In addition, when considering the adoption of a curriculum, the objectives, goals, and outcomes of the unit must be aligned like the human backbone. The goals/objectives drive the learning tasks leading to outcomes. While the progression through these elements may not remain linear for some learners, the connections must be there to guarantee high quality learning and cognitive growth in gifted students.

In Practice

In one building, kindergarten teachers worked together with a gifted resource teacher to create a unit on desert animals. The resource teacher first aligned the unit with the standards that were already a part of the kindergarten curriculum, then as a team they selected learning goals for the unit. One enduring understanding for the unit was that all living things in the desert biome must adapt to changes in their environment. The gifted resource teacher then helped align her task with both the needs of her students and the needs of the grade level. She came up with a performance task for the end of the unit that would challenge students to approximate the practice of a scientist called "Ask an Expert."

Ask An Expert:

In our groups today, the class will be finding out how an ecologist would organize animals for study. They will work in groups to create proposals for the study. Just like a real scientist, they will need to include the cost of field research.

Our rationale: This activity is designed to mirror a scientist seeking funding for research so the group needs to include those elements a scientist would include in a proposal such as a rationale and estimated costs of the research. Scientists are concerned about making sure that they persuade an organization that their research will further the study of ecology. They will create a rationale for the study based on their learning about adaptations and biodiversity and the need for both in order for a desert biome to thrive.

All groups will receive a "grant proposal" worksheet, pencils, and a variety of pictures of animals from the desert. Guidance for an authentic research question will vary.

Possible examples of research questions:

-What can we do to preserve the habitat of_____?

-How does this animal adapt to its changing environment?

The culminating activity for this unit will be the "research conference" that each group will attend to present the findings from their funded research. Parents and students are all invited to the conference presentations on the last day.

THE FUTURE STATE OF CURRICULUM

In the age of standards and accountability, we must consider how nationally developed standards fit students with gifts and talents. While many of the qualities found in national standards (e.g., Common Core State Standards, Next Generation Science Standards, Social Studies, technology and so on) require students to use content and skills to demonstrate learning and have focused on increased rigor and challenge, this may not always be sufficient for gifted students. While standards identify a target, for some students this target is too easy to hit. We must look at standards as a guide for what students need to know, understand, and be able to do and adjust our target goals to meet the learning strengths and needs of the gifted students we serve.

Defining Rigor

In order to meet the learning needs of all students, and particularly students with gifts and talents, we must also consider how the curriculum selected provides rigor and challenge in order for all learners to reach their potential. Rigor and relevance are two terms used in many discussions of standards and accountability. But what do we mean by the term rigor? The glossary of education reform defines rigor as tasks that encourage students to think critically; are academically, intellectually, and personally challenging; and help students understand concepts that are complex and ambiguous. Rigorous learning experiences ask students to question their assumptions and think deeply. Academically rigorous learning experiences should challenge an individual or group to learn more and in greater depth. One idea to remember is that rigor and hard are NOT the same thing nor do they promote the same outcome. Rigorous tasks are challenging and bring students to a level of engagement where students and content interact. Hard can be out of reach for an individual and can lead to disengagement, frustration, and discouragement. What we want in a curriculum for the gifted is rigor that engages, challenges, and develops student thinking.

In response to standards (i.e., Common Core State Standards, or any other standards uniformly applied) we must consider how they may need to be adjusted to meet particular students' needs. For some students, these standards may need modification that includes acceleration of students' learning, alteration of task demands to provide appropriate challenge, building greater interdisciplinary connections and/or providing gifted students the opportunity to work with several standards at the same time. Further, enhanced standards should promote the development of authentic assessments to evaluate student outcomes matched to the advanced levels of performance and growth of our gifted students.

Curriculum Appropriate for Advanced Students

When creating a curriculum unit for use with gifted students, teachers must include advanced content that is differentiated to meet student readiness, interests, and learning profiles. It should also require students to explore ideas in greater depth and in a more complex manner, offering opportunity for developing student talent. Ideally, a quality unit of study should promote authentic performances/products produced for a real-world audience, causing students to reflect on their own learning and to make interdisciplinary connections either through themes, concepts, generalizations, or ideas. While these ideas can be challenging for a curriculum writer, they ensure appropriate learning opportunities are available to gifted students since they are aimed at fostering maximum growth.

The creation of curriculum is not an easy task and to create units for gifted students demands even more of the curriculum writer. In reviewing the expectations of NAGC Gifted Programming Standards for Pre-K-12 students[15], the need for learner centered, divergent processes, and authentic products and audience are important components to consider. The NAGC Curriculum Studies Network has an annual competition for outstanding units for gifted students served in both gifted classroom and in heterogeneous classroom placements. Units are reviewed using a 3-point scale rubric that has met high inter-rater reliability based on three years of reviews[16] (See Figure 1). This rubric incorporates the elements of what is expected in an exemplary unit and can serve as a checklist for reviewing published curricula or it can serve as a guide as you construct your own curriculum.

Figure 1. NAGC Curriculum Studies Network Revised Rubric for Rating Curricular Material in 12 Key Areas

---

This figure delineates the key features and what is expected in an exemplary unit.

I. Nature of Differentiation

Score of 1: Open-ended activities are included in the unit and allow for students differing needs

Score of 3: Activities and assignments that accommodate the learning needs of high achieving students are explicitly described. These include adjustments to content, process, product based on student readiness, interest, and learning profile throughout the unit.

NOTE: A unit with a score of 1 requires the inclusion of open-ended activities to address student-learning needs as a minimum for gifted curriculum. A unit with a score of 3 requires many more specific adjustments be used to address learning needs from Content, Process, and Product based on interest, readiness and learning profile.

II. Opportunities for Talent Development

Score of 1: The unit includes at least three of the activities below:

--Opportunities for "kid watching" and "talent spotting

--Opportunities for students to engage in some activities aligned with their individual strengths, preferences, or interests

--Opportunities to foster the connection between unit activities and potential career fields, leadership opportunities, or real-world applications

--Opportunities to interact with role models, community resources, mentors, or professionals in the field

--Opportunities to explore advanced content in that field

--Opportunities to acquire the skills, methodologies, and dispositions of the practicing professional in that field

--Opportunities to investigate real-world problems and to develop authentic products and services in that field

Score of 3: The unit uses multiple opportunities for talent spotting, uses data from these activities to drive future instruction AND includes student self-reflection on how tasks impacted their learning/perception of self as a learner.

NOTE: A unit with a score of 1 requires a minimum of 3 ways to develop the talent in students. A unit with a score of 3 requires not only multiple talent development opportunities but also must show evidence of student self-reflection, building the lifelong learner and intrapersonal awareness within students.

III. Clarity of Objectives

Score of 1: Objectives are stated but require assumptions on the part of the reviewer as to the outcome goals.

Score of 3: Objectives are clearly stated, specific, and unambiguous.

NOTE: The difference between a unit earning a score of 1 and 3 is the level of specificity and clear documentation of the outcome goals for the unit.

IV. Nature of the Objectives

Score of 1: The objectives are aligned to state and/or national standards. They are concerned with details and factual knowledge and include basic skill requirements.

Score of 3: Objectives are aligned to state and/or national standards and focus on students' learning and incorporating concepts, principles, cognitive skills, methodologies, and dispositions within a field of study.

NOTE: A unit with a score of 1 has a greater focus on basic knowledge/skills of the objectives. A unit with a score of 3 would demonstrate working with the ideas and skills of a discipline/field requiring students to do the work of a practicing professional including using the language of the discipline.

V. Evaluation Components

Score of 1: The assessment model is limited to paper and pencil evaluation instruments (i.e., tests, quizzes)

Score of 3: The assessment model includes at least three different evaluation measures including, for example, student portfolios, observational checklists of student behaviors, product evaluation, or self or peer evaluation. Assessment data is used to monitor student growth, provide student feedback, allow for student self-reflection, or to differentiate content or instruction.

NOTE: A unit with a score of 1 uses traditional assessment tools such as tests and quizzes. A unit with a score of 3 utilizes many different types of assessment to document student growth as well as use these assessments to provide students with quality feedback (rubrics and comments) as well as help teachers plan based on student performance.

VI. Learning Activities

Score of 1: Learning activities within the unit support different learning profiles and readiness levels.

Score of 3: Learning activities within the unit provide opportunities for student centered, problem based/real world application learning.

NOTE: A unit with a score of 1 would include methods to differentiate for student learning profiles and readiness. A unit with a score of 3 would have learning activities that reflect the work in a real world setting and are structured to be student centered thus making a powerful connection between what is learned and the engagement of the student.

VII. Instructional Strategies

Score of 1: The instructional strategies are described and provide opportunities for concept and methodology of a field exploration.

Score of 3: Instructional strategies require students to apply concepts and methodologies to address a real world problem.

NOTE: A unit with a score of 1 would include concepts and methods of the field of study represented in the unit. A score of 3 not only have the concepts and methods of the field within the unit but require students to apply these concepts and methods to address a real world problem.

VIII. Student Product and Assignments

Score of 1: The author describes a minimum of three different options for student products or assignments. The majority of these assignments involve convergent thinking, recall, and practice.

Score of 3: The author describes different kinds of student products or open-ended assignments, including the development of student driven creative products, or the development of products related to real-world applications or problem solving.

NOTE: A unit with a score of 1 does provide student choice with assignment options. A unit with a score of 3 provides choice but the assignments are open and require students to wrestle with the content to develop a product that provides a solution to a problem or reflects the work of the field in the real world.

IX. Resources and Level of Student Engagement with the Materials

Score of 1: The unit contains primary and secondary information sources to support student learning.

Score of 3: Students engage with resources that are authentic to the discipline/field of the unit. Students find and use appropriate resources to answer questions and solve problems authentic to the discipline/field of the unit.

NOTE: While a score of 1 requires the use of primary and secondary sources as a minimum expectation, a score of 3 requires student to not only use but find resources that are authentic to the field and use these resources to solve a problem that is authentic to the field, doing the work of a practicing professional.

X. Alignment of Curricular Components

Score of 1: The curriculum unit contains at least 5 lessons, each lesson describing the following instructional components: Objectives, Assessment, Introduction, Teaching strategies, Learning activities, Products, Resources, Differentiation strategies, and Talent development activities

Score of 3: The curriculum unit is clearly sequenced, is aligned to support learners, and provides options for increasing rigor and challenge to meet students' different learning needs.

NOTE: A score of 1 requires a unit to have the basic components of a lesson and includes the use of differentiation and talent development. A score of 3 requires these basics but specifically identifies the increase of rigor and challenge levels be embedded within the unit to support gifted student growth.

XI. Evidence of Effectiveness

Score of 1: The unit has been used at least once with students; anecdotal evidence is included such as teacher impressions of success.

Score of 3: The unit has been taught more than once. Developers describe a systematic effort to assess growth and change in gifted education students. This includes a clear plan for documenting student growth/change with work examples provided (actual student products and/or photos of student work). Reflections on effectiveness with students are provided and utilized to drive unit revisions.

NOTE: While there is a minimum expectation for use of a unit to identify areas needing possible revision, a   score of 1 notes evidence is more subjective in nature with the inclusion of impressions of effectiveness. A score of 3 requires multiple usesof a unit as well a planned way of documenting student growth – the use of student products and student reflection on the experience as a tool for unit revisions

XII. Ease of Use by Other Educators

Score of 1: Unit components are explained so teachers could implement it easily within their classroom setting.

Score of 3: Unit components are explicit; well sequenced and support teachers in differentiating learning within the unit tasks. Reflections on field test results are included as data driven revision suggestions for planning, implementation and use by others.

NOTE: Units with a score of 1 must be clear so teachers can easily use it in a variety of classroom settings. Units with a score of 3 explicitly document how teachers can differentiate learning tasks and show evidence of how data was used to revise the unit to make it easier for teachers to differentiate within the learning experiences in the unit.

CONCLUSION

Curriculum is at the heart of learning, what is desired for students, and what students want to know, understand and be able to do. When thinking about quality curriculum we must look for learning opportunities that ask students to explore complex questions, analyze issues surrounding an event with the intent of finding patterns and trends, judge with criteria, examine details and so on, master important skills, and build a strong desire for him/her to learn more. When we address these key features then learning is real, consuming, and exciting. But what must be in place for these types of opportunities to occur?

When writing or selecting a high quality curriculum, some key features must be present. First, differentiation must be an infused in the lessons, not as an add-on but as fibers within the fabric of the lesson design. This means not only making changes for students who may struggle, but also for all the variations of learning needs of those who are performing at a level above the grade to which they are assigned. It is important to remember to consider learners based on their readiness, interest, and learning profile in this process and to determine where we will make the changes to the content, process, and/or product. High quality curricula are vehicles for ensuring we match learners' readiness for challenge with the instructional tasks we pose.

Second, the learning tasks should provide opportunities that support talent development in all students. High quality curriculum units should include opportunities for talent spotting while students are working, posing questions, and developing products that can indicate areas of excellence within that child. This is important because not all students demonstrate their gifts and talents in the same way, in the same subjects, or at the same time. High quality curriculum provides a variety of learning options so students have the opportunity to bring gifted behaviors to the surface.

Third, the learning goals and evaluation tools must be aligned and embedded in learning tasks so a seamless connection exists between the two. One cannot measure what one has not clearly defined. High quality units should demonstrate this connection and provide the teacher and the students a clear road map for learning. The term road map does not suggest that all students must complete the same task but rather all students will demonstrate mastery of the learning goals at their readiness level as measured by an aligned evaluation tool.

Fourth, instructional strategies and activities must provide the "right fit" for each learner. If the learning tasks "fit" the student's zone of proximal development and the strategies used support students in gaining knowledge and skills, productive learning is more likely to be in place. High quality curriculum units provide opportunities to use different types of activities and strategies to meet students' learning needs and establish an engaging classroom experience.

Finally, within a quality curriculum, lesson products (outcomes) require students to make sense of the content or show how they can relate to the content, and apply what they learned in an authentic way. When outcomes are authentic (real world) individuals are more likely to participate at higher levels of performance. High quality curriculum units provide a variety of product types so different pathways can be explored and students can begin to practice producing in ways that mirror professionals in the discipline.

ENDNOTES

[1] National Governors Association & Council of Chief State School Officers. (2010). *Myths v. facts about common core standards*. Retrieved from http://www.corestandards.org/

[2] Hattie, J. A. C. (2009). *Visible learning: A synthesis of over 800 meta-analyses relating to achievement*. New York, NY: Routledge.

[3] Bransford, J., Brown, A., & Cocking, R. (Eds.). (2000). *How people learn: Mind, brain, experience, and school* (Exp. ed.). Washington, DC: National Academies Press.

[4] Kaplan, S. N. (2009). Layering differentiated curricula for the gifted and talented. In F. A. Karnes & S. M. Bean (Eds.), *Methods and materials for teaching the gifted* (3rd ed., pp. 107-135). Waco, TX: Prufrock Press.

[5] Kaplan, S. N. (2009).

[6] Tomlinson, C. A. (2014). *The differentiated classroom: Responding to the needs of all learners* (2nd ed.). Alexandria, VA: ASCD.

[7] Reis, S. M., Burns, D. E., & Renzulli, J. S. (1992). *Curriculum compacting: The complete guide to modifying the regular curriculum for high ability students*. Mansfield Center, CT: Creative Learning Press.

[8] Renzulli, J. S., & Reis, S. M. (1997). *The schoolwide enrichment model: A how to guide for educational excellence* (2nd ed.). Mansfield Center, CT: Creative Learning Press.

[9] Beasley, J. G. (2011). Preserving our identity: Learning about the history of our State. In M. B. Imbeau (Ed.), *Parallel Curriculum Units for Grades K-5* (pp. 153-194). Thousand Oaks, CA: Corwin Press.

[10] Wiggins, G. & McTighe, J. (2005). *Understanding by design* (2nd ed.). Alexandria, VA: ASCD.

[11] Passow, A. H. (1979). *The gifted and the talented: Their education and development*. Chicago, IL: University of Chicago Press.

[12] Tomlinson, C. A., Kaplan, S. N., Renzulli, J. S., Purcell, J. H., Leppien, J. H., Burns, D.E. . . . Imbeau, M.B. (2009). *The parallel curriculum model* (2nd ed.). Thousand Oaks, CA: Corwin Press.

[13] Imbeau, M.B. (2011). *Parallel Curriculum Units for Grades K-5*. Thousand Oaks, CA: Corwin Press.

[14] VanTassel-Baska, J. (2003). Content-based curriculum for high-ability learners: An introduction. In J. VanTassel-Baska & C. A. Little (Eds.), *Content-based curriculum for high-ability learners* (pp. 1-23). Waco, TX: Prufrock Press.

[15] National Association for Gifted Children. (2010). *NAGC pre-K-grade 12 gifted education programming standards: A blueprint for quality gifted education programs.* Retrieved from http://www.nagc.org.

[16] Purcell, J.H., Burns, D.E., Tomlinson, C.A., Imbeau, M.B., Martin, J.L. (2002). Bridging the gap: A tool and technique to analyze and evaluate gifted education curricular units. *Gifted Child Quarterly*, 46, 306-321.

KEY RESOURCES FOR PARENTS AND EDUCATORS

For units using the **Integrated Curriculum Model**, the following list can be helpful. This does not represent all units, but highlights a few in different grade levels as well as subjects.
Beyond Words: Grades 1-2. Kendall Hunt (2011).
Journeys and Destinations: Grades 2-3. Kendall Hunt (1998).
Beyond Base Ten: A Mathematics Unit for High-Ability Learners, Grades 3-6. Prufrock Press (2008).
Moving Through Dimensions: A Mathematics Unit for High Ability Learners, Grades 6-8. Prufrock Press (2010).

For units using the **Multiple Menu Model**, the following example is just one that parents and educators can refer to when exploring this model.
Real Patriot Games: A Unit Study on Intelligence and Espionage Based on the Multiple Menu Model. Prufrock Press (2006).

For more information on developing units using the Multiple Menu Model, please refer to:
Renzulli, J. S., Leppien, J. H., & Hayes, T. S. (2000). *The multiple menu model: A Practical Guide for Developing Differentiated instruction*. Waco, TX: Prufrock Press.

For a series of units using the **Parallel Curriculum Model**, the following provide examples in a variety of grade levels and subjects. All are available from Corwin Press, Thousand Oaks, CA.
Parallel Curriculum Units for Grades K-5 (2011).
Parallel Curriculum Units for Science, Grades 6-12 (2011).
Parallel Curriculum Units for Mathematics, Grades 6-12 (2011).
Parallel Curriculum Units for Language Arts, Grades 6-12 (2009).
Parallel Curriculum Units for Social Studies, Grades 6-12 (2010).

For more information on developing units using the Parallel Curriculum Model, please refer to:

Tomlinson, C. A., Kaplan, S. N., Renzulli, J. S., Purcell, J. H., Leppien, J. H., Burns, D.E. . . . Imbeau, M.B. (2009). *The parallel curriculum model* (2nd ed.). Thousand Oaks, CA: Corwin Press.

NAGC Website Resource for Award-winning Curriculum
http://nagccurriculumnetwork.weebly.com/
This website archives the NAGC Curriculum Award winners and provides links to either their published units or a contact email where you can find out more about their unit. There is also information about the award and how anyone can enter the challenge.

If you are looking for resources on how **curriculum for the gifted and Common Core State Standards** work together, the following resources can get you started:

Johnsen, S. K., & Sheffield, L. J. (Eds.). (2013). Differentiating the Common Core State Standards for gifted and advanced students. In *Using the Common Core Standards for mathematics with gifted and advanced learners* (pp. 12-23). Waco, TX: Prufrock Press.

Van Tassel-Baska, J. (Ed.). (2013). Differentiating the Common Core State Standards for gifted and advanced students. In *Using the Common Core Standards for English/Language Arts with gifted and advanced learners* (pp. 7-29). Waco, TX: Prufrock Press.

ABOUT THE AUTHORS

Dr. Jennifer Beasley is currently an Assistant Professor in Curriculum and Instruction at the University of Arkansas where she teaches courses in the Masters of Arts in Teaching program. Her professional contributions include serving as a regular columnist for the National Association for Gifted Children's publication Teaching for High Potential as well as Chair for the Curriculum Studies Network. Her research interests include: student engagement, teacher efficacy, curriculum design and differentiated instruction

Dr. Christine Briggs is an Associate Professor and Center for Gifted Education Director at the University of Louisiana at Lafayette. Her professional contributions include: Chair of the NAGC Curriculum Award and member of the NAGC awards committee. Her research interests include: under-representation of diverse students, curriculum design and differentiated instruction.

Leighann Pennington currently teaches gifted students through intensive online courses. She earned a B.A. in English from Miami University and M.Ed. in Educational Psychology and Gifted Education from the University of Virginia. Her articles are published in NAGC's Parenting Gifted Children, Teaching for High Potential, and Parenting for High Potential.

Dr. Marcia B. Imbeau is currently a Professor in the Department of Curriculum and Instruction at the University of Arkansas where she teaches in the childhood education and special education programs. Her research interests include: differentiated instruction, curriculum development, gifted education, pre-service teacher education, student engagement, and action research.

ABOUT THE SERIES EDITOR

Cheryll M. Adams, Ph.D., is the Director Emerita of the Center for Gifted Studies and Talent Development at Ball State University. She has served on the Board of Directors of NAGC and has been president of the Indiana Association for the Gifted and the Association for the Gifted, Council for Exceptional Children.